D1499752

COUNTRY PROFILES

KENYA

BY AMY RECHNER

BELLWETHER MEDIA • MINNEAPOLIS, MN

Blastoff! Discovery launches
a new mission: reading to learn.
Filled with facts and features, each
book offers you an exciting new
world to explore!

This edition first published in 2019 by Bellwether Media, Inc.

No part of this publication may be reproduced in whole or in
part without written permission of the publisher.
For information regarding permission, write to Bellwether
Media, Inc., Attention: Permissions Department,
6012 Blue Circle Drive, Minnetonka, MN 55343.

Library of Congress Cataloging-in-Publication Data

Names: Rechner, Amy, author.
Title: Kenya / by Amy Rechner.
Description: Minneapolis, MN : Bellwether Media, Inc., 2019.
    | Series: Blastoff! Discovery: Country Profiles | Includes
    bibliographical references and index.
Identifiers: LCCN 2018039002 (print) | LCCN 2018039675
    (ebook) | ISBN 9781681036793 (ebook) | ISBN
    9781626179615 (hardcover : alk. paper)
Subjects: LCSH: Kenya–Juvenile literature.
Classification: LCC DT433.522 (ebook) | LCC
    DT433.522.R43 2019 (print) | DDC 967.62–dc23
LC record available at https://lccn.loc.gov/2018039002

Editor: Rebecca Sabelko   Designer: Brittany McIntosh

Printed in the United States of America, North Mankato, MN.

TABLE OF CONTENTS

MASAI MARA
NATIONAL RESERVE

An hour before dawn, a family of **tourists** wakes
to the sound of a lion's roar outside their campsite's
gate. They get ready for a wildlife **safari** inside Masai
Mara National **Reserve**! They head out with their
guide. Cameras click as the family comes upon giraffes
nibbling leaves.

OTHER TOP SITES

FORT JESUS

LAKE VICTORIA

MOUNT KENYA

NAIROBI NATIONAL MUSEUM

They see lionesses chasing zebras across the **savanna** and rhinos cooling off at a watering hole. Herds of antelope, wildebeest, and red elephants fill the open **plains**. As they head back to their campsite, dry grasses seem to shimmer in the heat of the afternoon. This is Kenya!

5

LOCATION

Kenya is located along the **equator** in East Africa. It covers about 224,081 square miles (580,367 square kilometers). The capital city of Nairobi sits in the south-central part of the country just south of the equator.

Kenya's neighbor to the east is Somalia. The Indian Ocean washes upon Kenya's southeastern shore. Tanzania spans across the southern border while Lake Victoria, Africa's largest freshwater lake, lines the southwest corner. Uganda is to Kenya's west. South Sudan and Ethiopia are its neighbors to the north.

SOUTH SUDAN

UGANDA

NO DAYLIGHT SAVING TIME!

Because Kenya is on the equator, it gets the same amount of daylight all year long. Seasonal changes in the Earth's tilt do not affect Kenya the way countries farther north or south are affected.

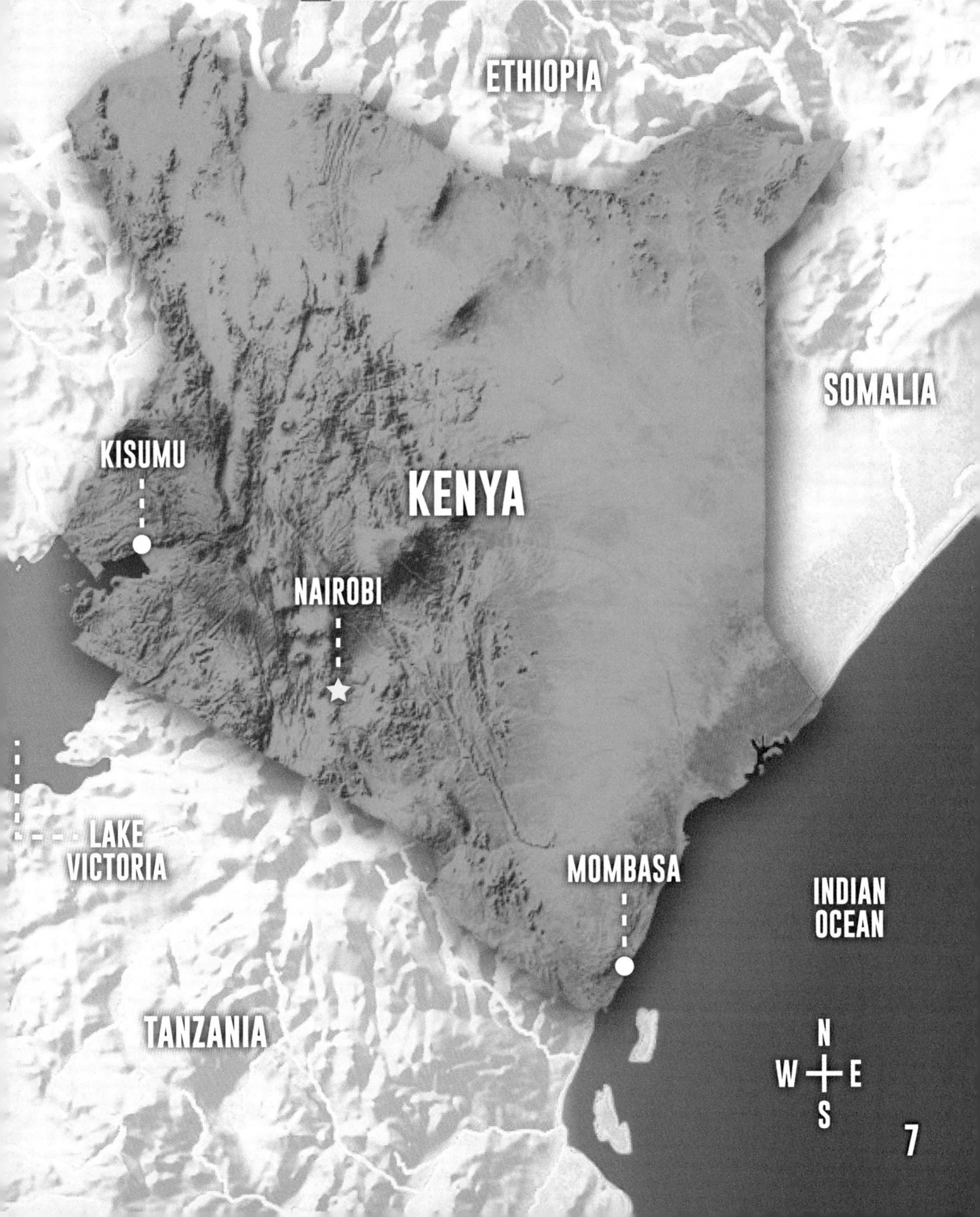

ETHIOPIA

SOMALIA

KISUMU

KENYA

NAIROBI

LAKE VICTORIA

MOMBASA

INDIAN OCEAN

TANZANIA

N
W E
S

LANDSCAPE AND CLIMATE

Kenya has a very **diverse** landscape. The eastern coast gives way to low plains. It is hot and humid with heavy spring rains. The **arid** Chalbi Desert blankets the north. Lake Turkana in the northwest corner is the world's largest desert lake. It glows green from its high salt content.

LAKE TURKANA

☐ = GREAT RIFT VALLEY
■ = CHALBI DESERT

N
W + E
S

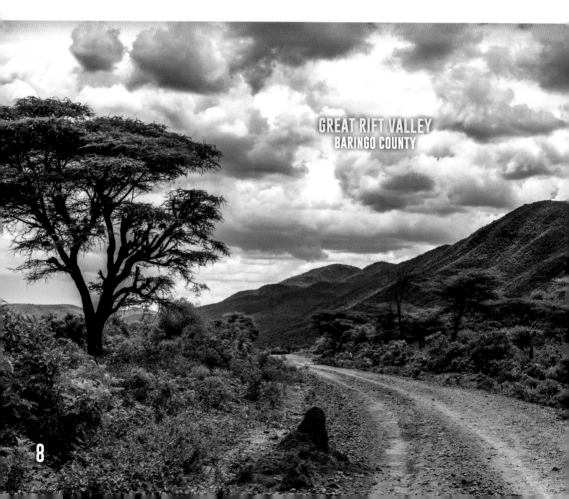

GREAT RIFT VALLEY
BARINGO COUNTY

MOUNT KENYA
MOUNT KENYA NATIONAL PARK

NAIROBI

Average
seasonal highs
and lows

JANUARY
HIGH: 83 °F (28 °C)
LOW: 54 °F (12 °C)

APRIL
HIGH: 82 °F (28 °C)
LOW: 60 °F (16 °C)

JULY
HIGH: 80 °F (27 °C)
LOW: 55 °F (13 °C)

OCTOBER
HIGH: 78 °F (26 °C)
LOW: 62 °F (17 °C)

°F = degrees Fahrenheit
°C = degrees Celsius

TRIPLE CROWN

Mount Kenya is the tallest mountain in
Kenya. Temperatures drop below freezing
on the three snow-topped peaks, while the
nearby city of Chogoria enjoys summery
weather down on the ground!

Heavy rains occur each spring and fall in Kenya's
central highlands. These highlands are split by the
Great Rift Valley, a giant crack that runs south across
Africa. Mountains rim the rift valley's eastern edge.
West of the valley are grasslands and Lake Victoria.
There, the weather is hot and mostly dry.

Some of the world's most interesting animals make Kenya's savanna their home. The savanna is a wildlife **conservation area** to protect the animals from hunters. Lions and cheetahs hunt wildebeests and gazelles that roam the savanna. Giraffes munch on leaves while yellow baboons rest in tree branches. Hippos wade in muddy watering holes.

Forests shelter black-and-white colobus monkeys that live high in the trees. Leopards creep silently along branches. Rhinos cool off in the shade. In the arid Great Rift Valley, tens of thousands of flamingos live on Lake Nakuru.

GAZELLES

HIPPOS

GIRAFFE

LIFE IN THE TREES

Black-and-white colobus monkeys spend their whole lives in the trees. They have two-part stomachs that help them digest the leaves and unripe fruit they eat. They even find enough water to survive.

CHEETAHS

CHEETAH

Life Span: up to 12 years
Red List Status: vulnerable

cheetah range = ◼

LEAST CONCERN	NEAR THREATENED	VULNERABLE	ENDANGERED	CRITICALLY ENDANGERED	EXTINCT IN THE WILD	EXTINCT

FAMILY TIES

Tribes have many clans or groups within them. Each clan is known for a special trait, such as pride or hard work.

MAASAI TRIBAL MEMBERS

More than 47 million people live in Kenya. Around 500,000 **refugees** from Somalia have also made Kenya their home. There are small groups of Europeans, Asians, and **Arabs**, as well as 47 **native** tribes. The largest tribe is the Kikuyu. The Samburu and the Maasai maintain their **traditions**.

Many people in Kenya are Christian. Others are Muslim. Some still follow their native faith. English and Kiswahili are the official languages of Kenya, but many tribes also speak their native languages.

FAMOUS FACE

Name: Wangari Muta Maathai
Birthday: April 1, 1940
Hometown: Nyeri, Kenya
Famous for: Created the Green Belt movement for environmental conservation and became the first African woman and environmentalist to win the Nobel Peace Prize in 2004

SPEAK KISWAHILI

ENGLISH	KISWAHILI	HOW TO SAY IT
hello	jambo	JOM-boh
goodbye	kwaheri	kwa-HEIR-ee
please	tafadhali	tah-fahd-HAH-lee
thank you	asante	ah-SAHN-tay
yes	ndiyo	in-DEE-yoh
no	hapana	hah-PAH-nah

NAIROBI

MOBILE HOMES

The Samburu tribe travels to find grass for their livestock. Their huts are made of sticks and animal skins. They are quick to set up and take down. The huts are arranged in a circle called a *manyatta*.

Kenyans are loyal to their tribes, but family is the most important thing in their lives. In **rural** areas, extended families share a **compound**. They have small huts made of mud brick with roofs of **thatch** or tin. They share a well, a shower, and an outhouse.

One in four Kenyans lives in an **urban** setting. Some live in tall apartment buildings or townhouses. There are some grand houses, too. Thousands crowd together in **slums**. They have no plumbing or electricity. Streets are crowded with traffic.

NAIROBI

Traditions vary amongst different **ethnic** groups in Kenya. But people are usually friendly and kind. Many enjoy visiting each other for Sunday afternoon tea. City guests bring flowers for their host. Rural guests bring foods like sugar or coffee. Gifts are presented in a *kiondo*, or woven bag.

KIKUYU TRIBAL MEMBERS

Some Kenyans wear Western-style clothing. Men may wear short-sleeve dress shirts and pressed pants. Women wear dresses or skirts with short-sleeve tops. They also wear traditional *kanga*, bright printed cloth that wraps around the body. Some tribes, such as the Maasai and Samburu, still wear traditional clothing.

Kenya provides free primary school for students from ages 6 to 14. Secondary school requires paying **tuition**, so not all students are able to stay in school. Many must leave to work and help the family. But some are able to continue school and go to college.

Most people work in **agricultural** jobs. The largest crops are tea, coffee beans, and plants for homes and gardens. Miners dig up limestone and soda ash. Factories make clothing or machines. Many people work in tourism, too. Jobs in hotels, safari tourism, and other visitor services are common.

MINING SODA ASH

FARMING TEA LEAVES

2016 OLYMPICS TRACK EVENT

Kenya is famous for its world-class runners. Kenyans have won marathons all over the world. They have won 93 Olympic medals in track, including 30 gold medals. Soccer is also a popular sport. Children play in soccer leagues. Tennis, basketball, and field hockey are common in city schools and clubs.

SOCCER

Many people in rural areas use their free time to garden, which provides food as well as relaxation. Kids often make up games with whatever is around. City dwellers enjoy movies and relaxing in parks. In Mombasa, they swim at the beaches.

SWIMMING

AJUA

What You Need:
- one empty egg carton
- two small bowls, like cereal bowls
- 36 dried beans, pebbles, or beads

How to Play:
1. Cut the top off the egg carton.

2. Place a cereal bowl on each end of the egg carton. Put three beans in each of the 12 carton cups. Each player owns the cups nearest them. The cereal bowl to each player's right is home.

3. Player One picks up the three beans from any cup on their side. Moving to the right, they drop one bean in each cup along the board. If they reach their bowl, they drop in a bean. If it is the last bean of the three that is dropped in their home bowl, they get a free turn.

4. Player Two takes their turn and repeats step 3. If a player drops their last piece into an empty cup on their own side, they can capture the pieces from the matching cup on their friend's side. Captured pieces are put in their home bowl.

5. The game ends when a player empties all six cups on their side. The player who still has beans on their side puts them all in their home bowl. The player with the most beans wins!

FINGER FOOD

Kenyans traditionally eat with their right hands. They pinch off a chunk of ugali, shape it, and use it as a scoop. But some families use forks and knives.

Kenya's **cuisine** relies on corn, greens, and fruit. *Ugali*, a cornmeal mush that hardens as it cools, is eaten with many meals. Stews are made of spinach or kale and cooked with other vegetables and beans to make a hearty lunch and dinner. *Sukuma wiki*, or collard greens, is a common side dish.

Beef, chicken, and goat meat are popular. Fish is served along the coast. A flatbread called *chapati* is served with meals. Kenya's fruit crops provide dessert. Juices and smoothies are sold by city street carts.

UGALI

SUKUMA WIKI

N'DIZI

Ingredients
non-stick cooking spray

8 bananas, peeled

1/2 cup water

4 ounces (1 stick) melted butter, in a pie plate

1/2 cup chopped peanuts or other chopped nuts, on a large plate or pie plate

Steps

1. Spray a pie plate with non-stick cooking spray. Put the bananas in the pie plate. With the help of an adult, microwave for 30 seconds. They will become softer.

2. Remove the plate from the microwave. Using tongs, take a banana and dip it in the melted butter, coating it on all sides. Then roll the banana in the nuts. Place the banana back in the pie plate and repeat with the other bananas.

3. Bake in the oven for 15 minutes at 375 degrees Fahrenheit (191 degrees Celsius).

4. Serve with ice cream. A little chocolate sauce would taste good, too!

Kenya takes pride in its **culture** and artistic **heritage**. In November, the Mombasa Carnival celebrates Kenya's diversity. Parade floats feature themes from Kenya's different tribes. Concerts, dancing, and food attract different tribes to the festival. Jamhuri Day on December 12 celebrates Kenya's independence from Britain with feasts, parades, and dancing.

Christian holidays are widely observed. At Christmas, families celebrate with services and carol singing at church and a feast with *nyama choma*, or roasted meat. They decorate with balloons and flowers. Faith and family fill Kenya's holidays with joy!

OFF TO THE RACES!

Camel races are the main attraction at the International Camel Derby and Festival! It takes place during the middle of the year in Maralal, a town in northern Kenya.

JAMHURI
DAY

25

TIMELINE

100 CE
Islamic Arabs trade along Kenya's coast

BEFORE 3000 BCE
Earliest known ancestors of humans believed to live in Kenya

1947
Jomo Kenyatta becomes leader of Kenya African Union (KAU) and starts a peaceful movement toward independence

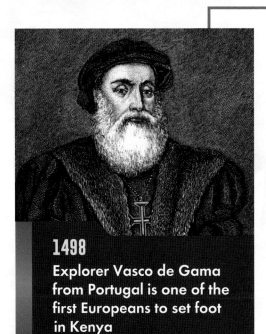

1498
Explorer Vasco de Gama from Portugal is one of the first Europeans to set foot in Kenya

1888
Britain gains control over Kenya

1963
Kenya becomes an independent nation

2018
Heavy rains reveal a 50-foot deep crack in Kenya's Rift Valley; scientists believe the crack may cause Africa to split apart in millions of years.

1952-56
Rebel KAU members who formed the Kikuyu fighters attack white settlements and farms

2000
Kenyans take first, third, and fourth places in the Boston Marathon

Official Name: Republic of Kenya

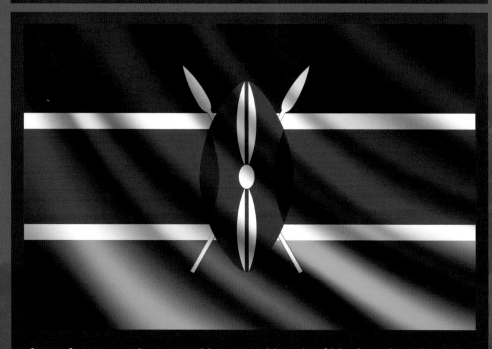

Flag of Kenya: Three equal horizontal bands of black, red, and green, with thin strips of white above and below the red. Black stands for the people, red for bloodshed in the struggle for freedom, green for natural wealth, and white for peace. A large Maasai warrior's shield over crossed spears sits in the center.

Area: 224,081 square miles
(580,367 square kilometers)

Capital City: Nairobi

Important Cities: Mombasa, Kisumu

Population:
47,615,739 (July 2017)

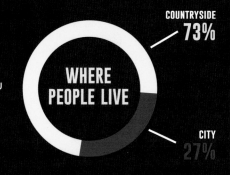

WHERE PEOPLE LIVE

COUNTRYSIDE
73%

CITY
27%

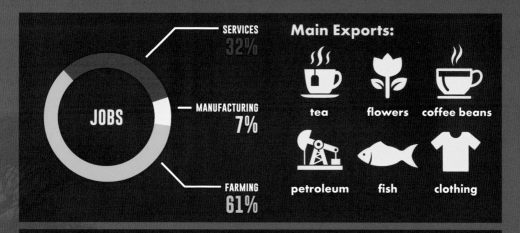

SERVICES
32%

Main Exports:

JOBS

MANUFACTURING
7%

FARMING
61%

tea   flowers   coffee beans

petroleum   fish   clothing

National Holiday:
Jamhuri Day (Independence Day)
(December 12)

Main Languages:
English and Kiswahili

Form of Government:
presidential republic

Title for Country Leaders:
president, deputy president

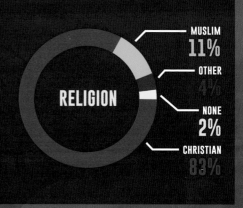

RELIGION

MUSLIM
11%

OTHER
4%

NONE
2%

CHRISTIAN
83%

Unit of Money:
Kenyan shilling

GLOSSARY

agricultural—related to the business of farming

Arabs—people who are originally from the Arabian Peninsula

arid—very dry, with little rainfall

compound—an enclosed area that includes a group of buildings

conservation area—an area of land that is protected and that cannot be built on or used for certain purposes

cuisine—a style of cooking

culture—the beliefs, arts, and ways of life in a place or society

diverse—made up of people or things that are different from one another

equator—an imaginary circle around the Earth equally distant from the north and south poles

ethnic—related to a group of people who share customs and an identity

heritage—the traditions, achievements, and beliefs that are part of the history of a group of people

native—originally from the area or related to a group of people that began in the area

plains—large areas of flat land

refugees—people who flee their homes for safety

reserve—land set aside to protect it

rural—related to the country and country life

safari—a journey

savanna—an African grassland containing scattered trees

slums—parts of cities that are crowded and have poor housing

thatch—a roof covering made of grass or straw

tourists—people who travel to visit another place

traditions—customs, ideas, or beliefs handed down from one generation to the next

tuition—money paid for instruction

urban—related to cities and city life

TO LEARN MORE

AT THE LIBRARY
Burgan, Michael. *Kenya*. New York, N.Y.: Children's Press, 2015.

Kras, Sara Louise. *Kenya: A Question and Answer Book*. Mankato, Minn.: Capstone Press, 2016.

Murray, Julie. *Kenya*. North Mankato, Minn.: Abdo Publishing, 2018.

ON THE WEB

FACTSURFER

Factsurfer.com gives you a safe, fun way to find more information.

1. Go to www.factsurfer.com.

2. Enter "Kenya" into the search box.

3. Click the "Surf" button and select your book cover to see a list of related web sites.

INDEX